The Young Geographer Investigates

Polar Regions

Terry Jennings

Oxford University Press 1986

Oxford University Press, Walton Street, Oxford OX2 6DP

Oxford   New York   Toronto
Delhi   Bombay   Calcutta   Madras   Karachi
Petaling Jaya   Singapore   Hong Kong   Tokyo
Nairobi   Dar es Salaam   Cape Town
Melbourne   Auckland

and associated companies in
Beirut   Berlin   Ibadan   Nicosia

Oxford is a trade mark of Oxford University Press

Oxford University Press 1986

ISBN 0 19 917075 4 (limp non-net)
ISBN 0 19 917081 9 (cased, net)

© Terry Jennings 1986

Typeset in Great Britain by
Tradespools Limited, Frome, Somerset
Printed in Hong Kong

Acknowledgements

The publishers would like to thank the following for permission to use transparencies:

B & C Alexander p.33 (bottom), p.37 (top right), p.38 (left and inset, bottom right); Arctic Camera/Derek Fordham: p.6 (top), p.26 (top), p.27 (top left), p.27 (bottom left), p.32 (centre right), p.33 (top), p.35 (bottom right); Ardea/S. Roberts: p.27 (bottom right); Ardea/P. Morris: p.30 (bottom right); Ardea/K. Fink: p.36 (bottom right); Aspect Picture Library: p.8 (bottom); Bruce Coleman/Jen and Des Bartlett: p.12 (right), Coleman/Jerry Hout: p.29 (bottom left), Coleman/Leonard Lee Rue III: p.30 (bottom left), Coleman/Wayne Lankinnen: p.30 (top right), Coleman/B & C Calhoun: p.31 (top right); Sir Ranulph Fiennes: p.17 (top); Susan Griggs/Michael Boys: p.10 (bottom right), Griggs/Tibor Hirsch: p.31 (left); Robert Harding Picture Library: p.37 (left) Eric and David Hosking: p.7 (top and bottom), p.13 (bottom right), p.14 (centre), p.15 (bottom), p.29 (top and bottom right); Terry Jennings: p.16 (top), p.46; Frank Lane Picture Agency/Christiana Carvalho: cover picture, p.10 (left), p.14 (top right), Frank Lane/Steve McCutcheon: p.27 (top right), p.28 (top and bottom left), p.31 (bottom right), p.34 (left and right), p.35 (bottom left and top right), Frank Lane/C. Rhodes: p.29 (top left), Frank Lane/Mark Newman: p.30 (top left); O.S.F./Doug Allan: p.4 (bottom), p.8 (2nd from bottom), p.10 (top right), p.11 (inset), p.13 (left and top right), O.S.F./Peter Parks: p.8 (top), O.S.F./Jill Bailey: p.9 (bottom); Bryan Sage: p.28 (bottom right), p.35 (bottom left inset); Science Photo Library/David Millar: p.15 (top); Seaphot/Planet Earth Pictures: p.12 (left); Spectrum Colour Library: p.32 (bottom left and top left), p.37 (bottom right); Charles Swithinbank: p.6 (bottom), p.9 (top), p.14 (bottom right), p.36 (top right)

Illustrations by Rudolph Britto Chapman Bounford Gary Hincks
Ed McLachlan Ben Manchipp Maggie Silver Paul Thomas
Ann Winterbotham Gerald Witcomb

Contents

The ends of the Earth

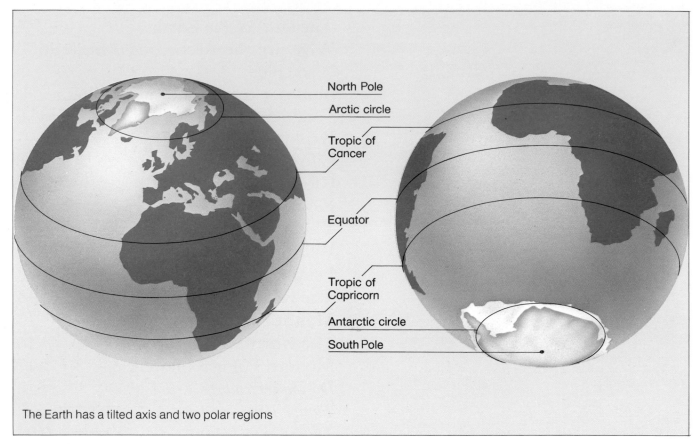

North Pole
Arctic circle
Tropic of Cancer
Equator
Tropic of Capricorn
Antarctic circle
South Pole

The Earth has a tilted axis and two polar regions

All the time our Earth is spinning round. It spins as if it were a giant top turning on an invisible axis. The upper end of this invisible axis is the North Pole. The bottom of the invisible axis is the South Pole.

This book is about these two ends of the Earth. It is about the places which are furthest away from the Equator. Sometimes these places are called the polar regions. This is because they are around the North and South Poles. Maps and atlases call these two ends of the Earth the Arctic and Antarctic. The Arctic is the area around the North Pole. The Antarctic is the area around the South Pole.

The Arctic and Antarctic were the last parts of the Earth to be explored and mapped. They are the coldest places on Earth. All the year round most of the ground is frozen solid and there is ice and snow over it. It is so cold that in winter a tear will freeze on your cheek when you're crying, and water poured from a jug freezes before it reaches the glass.

Icy wastes of Antarctica

4

Why are the Arctic and Antarctic so cold?

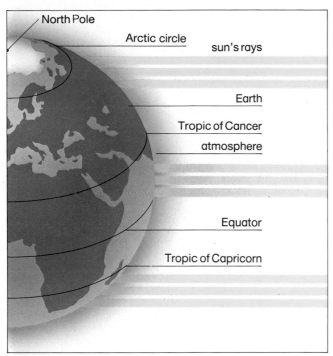

North Pole

Arctic circle

sun's rays

Earth

Tropic of Cancer

atmosphere

Equator

Tropic of Capricorn

Sunlight falls on the Equator and on the Polar Regions with different strengths.

All round the Earth is a layer of air. This layer of air is called the atmosphere. The sun's rays must pass through the atmosphere before they can warm the Earth. The sun's rays lose some of their heat as they pass through the air.

Around the centre part of the Earth called the Equator, the sun blazes down at right angles. The tropics receive hot sunshine all the year round. But the Poles are on a part of the Earth which is curved away from the sun. The sun's rays have to go further through the air. More of the sun's heat is lost and therefore the polar regions are cold.

In addition, when the Earth goes round the sun, the Earth is slightly tilted. It is this tilt of the Earth which gives us our seasons. For part of the year the North Pole is tilted away from the sun. Then it is winter at the North Pole (A). At the same time the South Pole is tilted towards the sun. Then it is summer at the South Pole (B). Six months later the North Pole is tilted towards the sun and it has its summer (C). The South Pole is then tilted away from the sun and is having its winter (D).

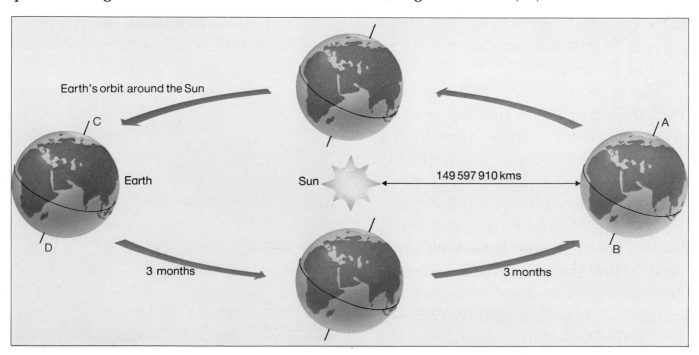

Earth's orbit around the Sun

C

Earth

Sun

149 597 910 kms

A

D

3 months

3 months

B

Summer and winter in the polar regions

Midnight in Greenland during the summer

In the middle of summer the sun never sets in the polar regions. That is why they are often called 'the lands of the midnight sun'. Summer in the Arctic brings temperatures as high as 27°C. In the Antarctic the temperature rarely rises above freezing point even in summer. But days of bright sunshine may melt a little of the snow.

The reason for these differences is that the Antarctic is mainly land, while the Arctic is water surrounded by land. The land warms up quickly but loses its heat quickly. Water warms up more slowly but holds its heat longer. In the Arctic, the Arctic Ocean holds its heat for a long time. And so the Arctic is slightly warmer. In Antarctica the land loses its heat quickly and ice and snow cover most of the ground, even in summer. The whiteness of the snow also reflects the heat of the sun back into space.

In the winter both the Arctic and Antarctic are bitterly cold. The temperatures may fall to −50°C or lower. In mid-winter the sun does not rise above the horizon. It is dark all day and all night in both the Arctic and Antarctic in mid-winter.

Polar ice in the sunlight at night

Exploring the Poles

The first person to reach the North Pole was the American Robert Peary. He had spent more than 20 years exploring the Arctic. He had already become the first person to discover that Greenland was an island. Peary made several attempts to reach the North Pole. Finally he arrived in 1909. He stood on the only spot on Earth where every path leads southwards.

In 1911 a Norwegian named Roald Amundsen set out to reach the South Pole. His team took with them sledges, skis and 52 Eskimo husky dogs. At about the same time an English explorer, Robert Scott, set out with a team of men to reach the South Pole. Scott did not believe in the value of sledge dogs. Instead he took pack horses and motor sledges to carry his men and equipment

Amundsen sent Scott a telegram challenging him to a race to the South Pole. But on the way Scott's motor sledges broke down. The pack horses collapsed. Amundsen arrived at the South Pole in December 1911. Scott reached the Pole a month later in January 1912. Amundsen returned safely. But on the way back Scott and his men all died from starvation and cold. And yet they were only 17 km from one of their food stores.

Robert Scott's route to the South Pole
(Inset above) Scott's hut at Cape Evans near Mount Erebus, Antarctica
(Inset below) Inside Scott's hut

BAY OF WHALES

QUEEN MAUD RANGE

AMUNDSEN'S ROUTE

DISCOVERY INLET

SOUTH POLAR PLATEAU

Amundsen

SOUTH POLE

Scott

SCOTT'S ROUTE

Scott

Life in the polar seas

Although there are not many kinds of living things on land, there are many living things in the polar seas. The cold polar seas contain a lot of oxygen which all living things need in order to live. Warmer currents flow towards the poles from places nearer to the Equator. These currents bring large amounts of mineral salts which living things need to grow.

The most common living things in the polar seas are tiny plants and animals. These are known as plankton. When the sun shines the tiny plants grow rapidly. The tiny animals feed on the tiny plants. These tiny animals in turn are eaten by fish, whales, birds, seals and other animals. Some of these creatures in turn are eaten by leopard seals and killer whales. In this way many of the larger animals in the Arctic and Antarctic depend directly or indirectly on plankton in the sea for food.

The way in which living things are linked together through their food is called a food chain.

A typical food chain: fish eat plankton, seals eat fish, and polar bears eat seals

Glaciers

Glaciers are rivers of ice. There are many glaciers in the polar regions. Glaciers begin on mountains. They begin when snow collects in a hollow. More snow falls and the snow at the bottom of the hollow is pressed into ice. The weight of snow and ice gradually spreads out into a tongue of ice.

This tongue of ice is a baby glacier. It begins to slide downhill. As the glacier flows downhill it is joined by other glaciers. Gradually the glacier gets bigger and bigger. The longest glacier in the world is the Lambert Glacier in the Antarctic. It is at least 402 kilometres long and up to 64 kilometres wide. The Lambert Glacier was discovered by the crew of an Australian aircraft in 1956.

As a glacier slides slowly down a hill or mountain, it cuts a wide valley shaped like the letter U. If the ice melts it leaves behind little hills of stone and soil. These were pushed along by the sliding ice. When a glacier reaches the sea, pieces break off it. These icebergs float away.

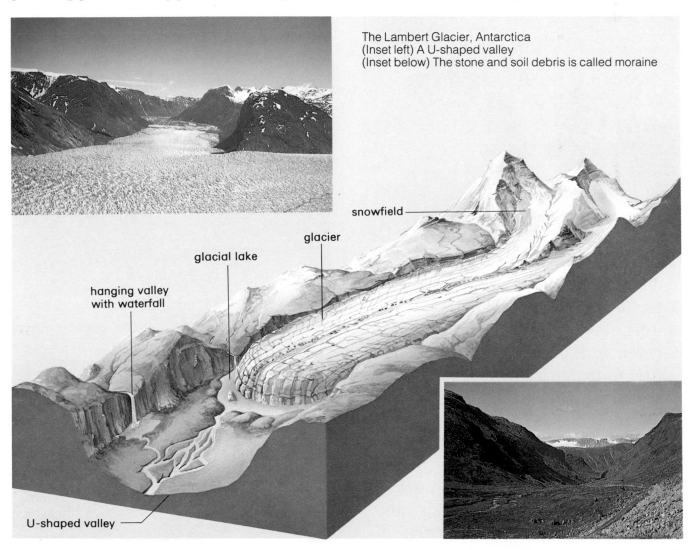

The Lambert Glacier, Antarctica
(Inset left) A U-shaped valley
(Inset below) The stone and soil debris is called moraine

snowfield

glacier

glacial lake

hanging valley
with waterfall

U-shaped valley

Floating ice

Icebergs are a big danger to ships that sail to the far north or south of the world. Not all icebergs are the same. Some icebergs come from glaciers on land. When these glaciers reach the sea, huge pieces of ice break off them and crash into the water. These icebergs are craggy and sharp. Only about one-eighth of an iceberg sticks up above the water. So if an iceberg towers 100 metres above the surface, it goes down 700 metres below the surface.

Flat-topped icebergs were once part of an ice-sheet

This craggy iceberg is about to break off a glacier

The other kind of iceberg is found around Greenland and in the Antarctic. In these places the land is covered with a huge sheet of ice. Each winter more ice is formed. This ice moves slowly down to the sea. Pieces break off the ends of these ice sheets and float away. These icebergs are huge and flat-topped.

Another danger to ships is pack ice. Whereas icebergs are freshwater which is frozen, pack ice is frozen seawater. In winter, large stretches of the sea freeze and have a crust of ice. When spring arrives this begins to melt. Cracks appear in the ice. Gradually it breaks up and floats away. It forms pack ice.

An ice-breaker ship moves through pack ice

The Antarctic

The Antarctic, or Antarctica, is the area at the southern end of the Earth. It has roughly twice the area of Australia. Antarctica is inside an imaginary line around the Earth called the Antarctic Circle. Almost at its centre is the South Pole.

As we have seen, the Arctic is a frozen ocean surrounded by land. But the Antarctic is a frozen continent surrounded by oceans. Antarctica is one of the seven continents of the world. Most of it is covered with a sheet of ice which is often about 2 kilometres thick. The snow that falls on Antarctica is gradually crushed into ice by the weight of fresh snow that falls on top of it. Most of this ice is slowly moving towards the edge of the land. It moves only a few metres a year. When the ice reaches the sea, it moves across the water as an ice shelf. The ice sticks up above the water like huge white cliffs.

Antarctica is much colder than the Arctic. The average temperature inland in Antarctica is −57°C. The winds often blow at 200 kilometres an hour. No plants and animals live on the land, except for a few penguins and seals near the sea.

The Brunt Ice Shelf. The cliffs in the photograph are 25 metres high

ANTARCTIC CIRCLE

LAMBERT GLACIER

SOUTH POLE

ROSS ICE SHELF

MT EREBUS

Wildlife in Antarctica

Antarctica is a huge frozen desert. Only mosses and lichens grow near the coast. These plants provide food and shelter for a few tiny insects.

But as we have seen, around the long coastline lies a rich ocean. The surface waters are alive with plankton. It is here, where the land meets the sea, that most wildlife is found. In the sea the plankton provides food for large numbers of fish. It also provides food for penguins, skuas, seals and whales.

Skuas eating a dead penguin

A leopard seal

The largest animal in the Antarctic is the blue whale. It is also the largest animal in the world. A blue whale can grow to be 30 metres long. It may weigh 100 tonnes, nearly as much as nine double-decker buses. And yet these huge creatures feed only on tiny plankton animals. Once blue whales were common in the Antarctic. But hunting has reduced the numbers of these wonderful animals. Now there are only a few thousand left in the whole world.

A blue whale

Penguins

The most common Antarctic creatures are the penguins. These birds are not able to fly. Their wings have evolved into flippers. Penguins use their wings to 'fly' through the water. They are able to swim under water as easily as most of the fish on which they feed.

A Gento penguin swimming

An Emperor penguin and a three-week-old chick

A penguin's body is covered with tiny oily feathers. These overlap like the tiles on a roof to keep out the water. Under these feathers is a layer of down and a thick layer of fat. These help to keep out the cold. The penguin's body is streamlined so that it can move under water like a torpedo. But on land penguins are quite clumsy. Some of them 'toboggan' over snowy slopes.

Some kinds of penguins build little nests of pebbles. The two largest kinds make no nest at all. Usually both the males and the females take turns in keeping the eggs warm until they hatch. The main enemy of penguins is the leopard seal. This hides under the ice waiting for the penguins to enter the water. Then the seal tries to catch and eat them.

Tobogganning penguins

13

The Ross Ice Shelf

The Ross Ice Shelf is a huge floating raft of ice. It is larger than France or Spain. There are several ice shelves in the Antarctic. But the Ross Shelf is the largest. It fills a bay on the coast of Antarctica. And it extends far out to sea.

An ice cave on the face of the Ross Ice Shelf

Ice cliffs of the Ross Ice Shelf

On its seaward edge the Ross Shelf consists of ice cliffs. These are 800 kilometres long and 60 kilometres high. From time to time these cliffs crack. Huge pieces of the ice break off and float away. Many of these icebergs are between 30 and 50 kilometres long. But the Ross Shelf does not get any smaller. All the time new ice is being added to it. Some of the ice comes from glaciers on the land. Some comes from frozen sea water. But most of the new ice is formed from the snow which falls on the Shelf.

Many expeditions to the South Pole started from the Ross Shelf. Both Roald Amundsen's and Robert Scott's expeditions started there. Today the United States and New Zealand have scientists living on the Ross Shelf. A few tourists ships visit the Ross Shelf as well.

A scientific expedition in the middle of the ice shelf

14

Mount Erebus

There are many extinct volcanoes in Antarctica. These are volcanoes which no longer erupt. But a few volcanoes are still active. One of these is Mount Erebus. It is 4024 metres high.

Although Mount Erebus is surrounded by ice and snow, steam is pouring from it all the time. Two or three times a day, lumps of molten rock, or lava, shoot out of its top or crater. Within this crater is a large lake. But this lake is not filled with water. It is filled with molten lava which bubbles and boils.

Near the rim of the Mount Erebus crater are geysers. These are springs which send out hot water. From time to time they shoot out hot water and steam into the cold Antarctic air. Elsewhere on Mount Erebus, hot gases escape into the air. These hot gases have made caves in the ice on the sides of the volcano.

A crater lake in Antarctica

The warm wet Antarctic

It seems that the polar regions were not always cold. One reason for believing this is that layers of coal 4 metres thick have been found in the Antarctic.

Coal was made from trees and other plants which grew millions of years ago. The trees and other plants died and were covered by mud and sand. The mud and sand pressed down on them. After millions of years the trees and other plants were turned into coal. So the Antarctic must have been much warmer and wetter for these trees and other plants to grow.

On the Earth there are seven huge land masses. These huge pieces of land are called continents. Antarctica is one of these continents. Long ago it is believed that all of the continents were joined together. They fitted together like the pieces of a jigsaw puzzle. It is thought that Antarctica was joined to Australia. Gradually the continents drifted apart. Australia drifted towards the hot tropics. But Antarctica drifted towards the bitterly cold South Pole.

Fossil fern found in coal

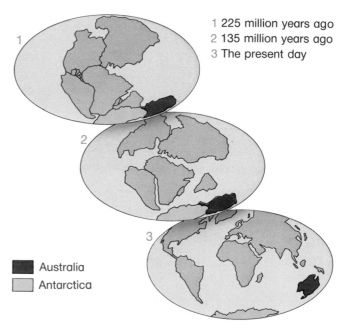

1 225 million years ago
2 135 million years ago
3 The present day

Australia
Antarctica

The ancient continent of Pangaea before it split into Antarctica and Australia

A swamp scene during the Carboniferous Period on Antarctica

Modern Polar Explorers

Ever since Peary first visited the North Pole, and Amundsen and Scott reached the South Pole, explorers have been going to these places. In August 1958, the American submarine *Nautilus* sailed under the ice of the Arctic Ocean. It sailed right underneath the North Pole. A year later another American submarine, *Skate*, sailed under the Arctic Ocean. The submarine stopped right underneath the North Pole. Then she floated upwards. She broke through the ice and became the first ship to reach the North Pole.

Fiennes on his transglobe expedition

In 1980 an expedition set out from Britain. It was led by the British explorer Sir Ranulph Fiennes. Over the next two years the team travelled right round the world. On the way, they crossed both the North and South Poles.

The discovery of valuable minerals in the polar regions has meant that more countries are taking an interest in them. The Antarctic has always been very difficult to explore. But several countries have permanent expeditions there. In 1959, 25 countries signed an agreement. They said they would use Antarctica only for peaceful scientific study. Now teams of scientists from 14 of these countries are living in the Antarctic. They are finding out more about this beautiful frozen continent.

Sir Ranulph Fiennes' route around the world

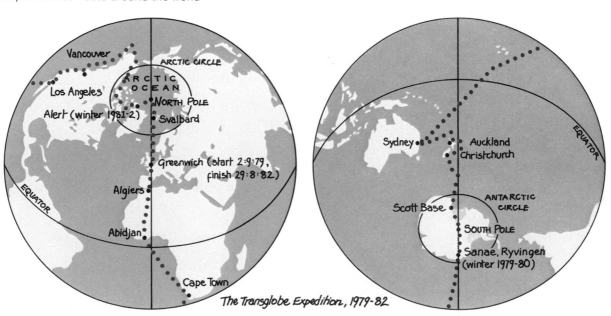

The Transglobe Expedition, 1979-82

Do you remember?

1 Where are the polar regions?

2 What happens to the sun's rays as they pass through the atmosphere?

3 What season is it at the North Pole when the North Pole is tilted away from the sun?

4 Why are the polar regions called the 'lands of the midnight sun?'

5 Why is the Antarctic colder than the Arctic?

6 Which cools down the quickest, the land or the sea?

7 Who was the first person to reach the North Pole?

8 Who was the first person to reach the South Pole?

9 What is plankton?

10 Name two kinds of animals or birds which eat plankton.

11 What is a food chain?

12 What is a glacier?

13 How and where do glaciers begin?

14 What is the shape of the valley cut by a glacier as it slides along?

15 What proportion of an iceberg sticks up above the water?

16 What are the two ways in which icebergs are formed?

17 What is pack ice?

18 How many continents are there?

19 How is the snow which falls on Antarctica turned to ice?

20 What are the only plants which grow in the Antarctic?

21 What is the largest animal in the Antarctic and what does it feed on?

22 What does a penguin use it wings for?

23 How does a penguin keep out the cold?

24 What is an ice shelf?

25 What is lava?

26 What is inside the lake at the top of Mount Erebus?

27 What is a geyser?

28 How do we know that the Antarctic used to be warmer?

29 What were the continents like long ago?

30 What did the countries who signed the agreement in 1959 say the Antarctic would be used for?

Things to do

1 Collect pictures of glaciers

Collect pictures of glaciers and how they have changed the landscape. Put your pictures in a book or on a wallchart. Write a sentence or two about each picture saying what it shows.

2 Use a thermometer

Ask your teacher to let you look at a thermometer. Handle it gently. It will break if you are not careful.

Use your thermometer to find the temperature of things. Try the temperature of the skin of your fingers, water from a tap, some ice or snow, the temperature in the middle of the playground on a sunny day and under the shade of a tree on the same day, and the temperature of the classroom. Ask your teacher to find the temperature of boiling water for you.

Take the temperature at the same spot in the playground at the same time every day. A good time would be 9 o'clock in the morning.

Make a graph showing how the temperature changes from day to day.

Hang a thermometer on a wall outside your classroom. Take the temperature every 30 minutes or every hour throughout one whole day.

Make a graph showing how the temperature changes. When is the hottest time of the day and when is it coldest?

In 1960 a temperature of −88°C was recorded in the Antarctic. How much lower is this than the lowest temperature you recorded outside your classroom?

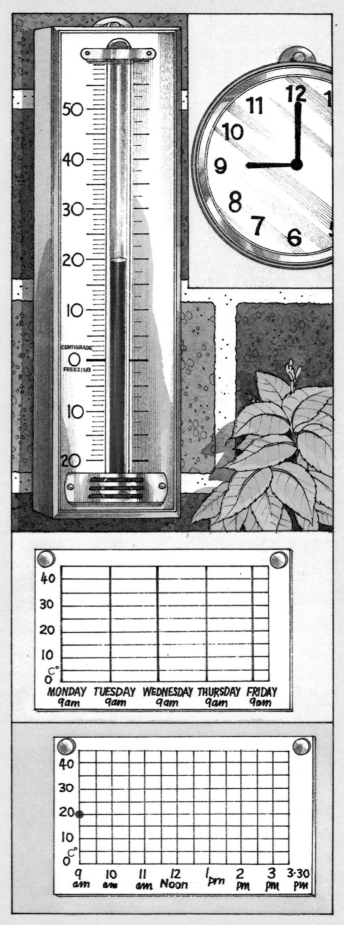

3 Looking at snowflakes   When it snows, catch a snowflake on a piece of black card. Look at your snowflake quickly with a hand lens or magnifying glass before the snowflake melts. If you have time draw your snowflake. Look at other snowflakes. Are they all the same?

4 Melting snow   Fill a jar with snow or pieces of ice. See how much water is formed when it melts. Which would form the most water, 5 centimetres of rain or 5 centimetres of snow?

Sprinkle some salt on ice or snow and see what happens. When do workmen do this?

5 Air in snow   How much air is there in snow which has fallen recently? Take a small clean tin. Fill the tin with water. Then pour this water into a measuring jug. How much water is there? This measurement is the tin's volume.

Gently push the tin, mouth downwards, into the snow until the tin is full. Stand the tin the right way up and wait until the snow melts. How much water is formed from a tin full of snow? The difference between the two volumes is the volume of air that was in the snow.

Can you think when the air in snow could be very useful to (a) people, (b) other animals?

6 Can you make ice from snow?   Find two tin cans, one a little smaller than the other. Pack sand or soil into the smaller can and put the lid on.

Fill the larger can with snow and put the smaller can on top of it. Press down on this smaller can with your foot. As you press, what happens to the snow? This is similar to what happens to the snow on a glacier. How is the snow pressed down there?

7 Freezing water Many people say that hot water freezes faster than cold water. Is this true?

Take two clean yoghurt pots. Fill one with hot water. Fill the other to the same level with cold water from the tap.

Put the two pots of water in a freezer or the freezing compartment of the refrigerator. Look at them every 30 minutes. Does the hot water or the cold water freeze first? Is the saying true?

9 How strong is ice? After a hard frost, collect a sheet of ice from a big puddle. Measure how thick the ice is.

Stand the sheet of ice over a bucket. Put weights on the ice. What weight can you add before the ice will break?

Try pieces of ice of other thicknesses. What is the strongest piece of ice you can find? How thick is it?

8 Melting ice cubes Take an ice cube from the refrigerator. How long does it take to melt in your classroom? How can you make an ice cube last longer outside the refrigerator? You might try wrapping ice cubes in newspaper, cloth, tissues and other materials. See which ice cube lasts longer. Perhaps you could have a competition with your friends to see who can make an ice cube last longest.

10 Life at the South Pole Pretend that you are living in a hut near the South Pole. Some scientists live for many months at a time in the Antarctic. Pretend that you are one of these scientists. Write a story describing what happens to you. Do not forget to say how you keep warm, how you obtain food and drink, and how you spend your days.

21

11 Make a model iceberg Make a model iceberg. Fill a yoghurt pot or a cream container with water. Put it in the freezing compartment of the refrigerator until the water is frozen solid.

Tear the container open and remove your model iceberg. Float it in a bowl of cold water. Measure how much of your iceberg is above the water. How much is below the water?

If you float your iceberg in a bowl of cold salty water, is there the same amount of it above and below the water?

12 Coconut ice Here is a recipe for some delicious coconut ice sweets. They will remind you of the ice of the polar regions. What is more, there is no cooking involved.

You will need:
8 tablespoons of condensed milk
350 grammes of icing sugar
175 grammes of desiccated coconut
A few drops of cochineal

1 Mix together the condensed milk and the icing sugar in a basin.

2 Stir in the coconut. The mixture should become very stiff.

3 Divide the mixture into two parts. Add a few drops of cochineal to one of the parts of the mixture. Stir it in thoroughly so that the whole mixture is pink.

4 Shape both parts of the mixture into bars, both the same size. Lay the white bar on top of the pink one and press them firmly together.

5 Dust a baking tray with icing sugar. Leave your coconut ice on this until it becomes firm.

6 Cut the bar of coconut ice into small squares ready to eat.

13 Kettle lakes

In some places where there are glaciers, huge pieces of ice become buried in the pieces of rock, soil and mud pushed along by the glacier. When these pieces of ice melt they often form water-filled hollows called kettle lakes.

It is easy to make some small kettle lakes. Just bury a few ice cubes in a pie dish of moist sand. Then level off the surface of the sand.

In time, what happens to the surface of the sand? Why is this?

14 Make a moss garden

There are hundreds of different kinds of mosses. They grow in all kinds of places including on walls, in cracks in pavements, on roofs, lawns, the bark of trees, damp soil and, of course, in the polar regions.

Almost any clear, uncoloured glass or plastic container can be turned into a moss garden – sweet jars, fish bowls and aquaria. Choose a container which is big enough to get you hands in.

Line the bottom of the container with clean shingle or small stones. On top of this put a thick layer of moist compost. Plant out some mosses, putting the taller ones towards the back and the shorter ones at the front. Arrange a few stones or pieces of rock amongst the mosses. Spray the mosses with water and then cover the container with cling-film or clear polythene which has air-holes made in it. Do not let the compost dry out, and spray the mosses with water from time to time.

A moss garden

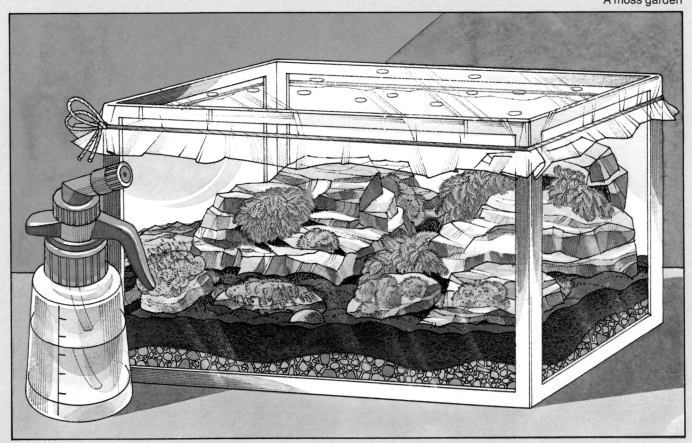

23

Things to find out

1   Find out how rain, snow and hail are formed.

2   Find out how long it takes for the Earth to travel right round the sun.

3   Why do you think it is that we do not feel the Earth spinning?

4   Look at an atlas. What three continents are partly inside the Arctic Circle?

5   From books in your school library, find out more about the lives of Peary, Amundsen, Scott and other polar explorers.

6   Why can glaciers move much larger pieces of rock than rivers can?

7   Find out why many glaciers have large cracks, called crevasses, breaking up their surfaces.

8   Some of the hotter parts of the world are seriously short of water. It has been suggested that tugs should tow icebergs from the Antarctic to these places to provide water. What disadvantages can you see in this idea?

9   Look at a map of Antarctica. Most of this continent is covered by ice. If all this ice melted, what would happen to the sea levels all over the world? What would happen to Antarctica itself? If the world became colder, what would happen to the Arctic and Antarctic? What would happen to the level of the sea?

10   Find out why whales are hunted. What is being done to save whales from becoming extinct?

11   Look at an atlas. Can you find any places which are just outside the Arctic and Antarctic circles? What kind of climates do these places have? Are there any large cities in these places? Find out all you can about them.

12   The four largest parts of Antarctica have been claimed by Australia, Britain, New Zealand and Norway. Why do you think these countries have claimed large parts of Antarctica?

13   Find out some of the food chains of which you are a member. Write out these food chains. What do you notice about the beginning of all food chains?

Food chain

14 One of the most famous ships to have been sunk by an iceberg was the ocean liner *Titanic*. Find out all you can about the sinking of the *Titanic*. When was she sunk, where, how many lives were lost? How big was the ship, how old was she? Why did the crash happen?

The Arctic

The Arctic is the name we give to the far northern part of the Earth. It is inside an imaginary circle around the Earth called the Arctic Circle. The Arctic Circle runs through Alaska, the northern tip of Canada, most of Greenland and northern Norway, Sweden and Finland. It also passes through Russia and a long strip of Siberia.

Within the Arctic Circle is the Arctic Ocean. This contains several large islands. The Arctic Ocean is five times the size of the Mediterranean Sea. But little water is to be seen. During the winter the Arctic Ocean is frozen over. In summer much of it is covered by pack ice.

Arctic iceberg off Greenland

The North Pole is at the centre of the Arctic Ocean. There is no land at the North Pole, only ice. In places the ice is as much as 3 kilometres thick. The lands around the Arctic Ocean are called the tundra. The tundra is a flat or gently sloping icy desert. And just below the surface the ground is always frozen, even in summer. This is called permafrost.

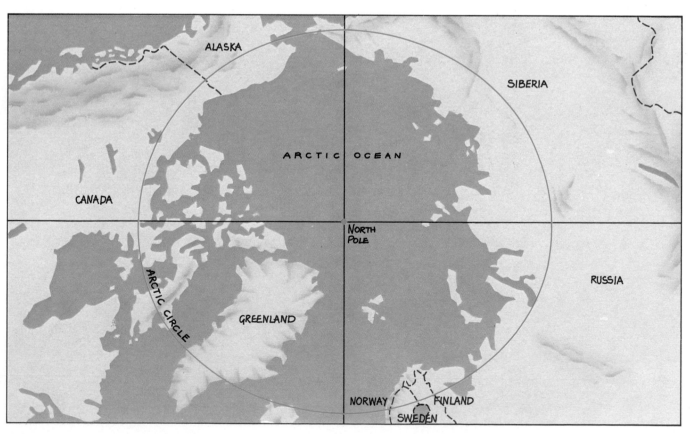

The Tundra

Heathers on the tundra

Reindeer moss

Very few plants grow in the Antarctic. But in the Arctic some plants manage to grow on the tundra. There are no trees on the tundra. It is too cold for them to grow. But there are some very small shrubs. These include heathers and dwarf willows and birches.

Summer on the tundra in Greenland

The most common plants in the drier areas are lichens. The most abundant of these is called 'reindeer moss', although it is really a lichen. This is the main food of several animals including reindeer and caribou. Mosses are common in the wetter areas on the tundra.

The other plants of the tundra are small and widely scattered. To anchor them against the strong winds they have long tap roots. The flowering plants often grow in a small cushion. Their leaves are usually leathery or waxy. This helps to stop the leaves losing water in the drying winds. All of these plants have to withstand being buried in snow and ice during the long Arctic winter.

Arctic poppies grow in small clumps

Permafrost

Marsh marigolds enjoy moisture and summer sunshine

On the tundra in summer much of the snow and ice melts. There is water everywhere. But about 30 centimetres below the surface the ground is permanently frozen. As we have seen, this permanently frozen ground is called permafrost. When the snow and ice melt at the surface in summer, the water cannot drain away. It cannot drain away because of the ice below the surface.

Permafrost

All over the tundra there are sharp pieces of rock. During the summer thaws, water seeps into cracks in the rocks. When it freezes the water expands or gets bigger. This weakens the rocks and makes them shatter. Gradually the rock breaks into smaller and smaller pieces because of the freezing and thawing.

The freezing and thawing sorts out the rocks into large and small pieces. The larger pieces of rock are pushed outwards. They settle out in circles or shapes called polygons. These shapes may be from a few metres to 100 metres across. Some of them are filled with water in summer.

Polygonal patterned ground

28

Animal life in the Arctic

The long dark winters and cold weather make life very difficult in the Arctic. But there are animals which have adapted to living there. One of these animals is the caribou. Tamed caribou are called reindeer. Caribou feed on lichens. They find these by scraping away the snow. When winter comes the caribou move further south.

Caribou

Another large animal of the tundra is the musk ox. The musk ox has a very thick coat to protect it from the biting cold winds. The musk ox is the only large animal to stay on the tundra throughout the winter. It feeds on mosses and grasses.

Musk oxen

The fiercest animal of the tundra is the polar bear. Its thick coat protects it from the cold. The polar bear's feet are covered with hair so that it can grip on the ice and snow. Polar bears eat some plants. But they feed mainly on fish, seals and birds.

Polar bear on an ice floe

The most numerous animals on the tundra are lemmings. There are millions of these small plant-eaters. The lemmings in turn are food for other, larger, animals and birds.

The prolific lemming

Arctic animals in winter

Only a few birds such as the ptarmigan and snowy owl live on the tundra all the year round. In the winter they grow thicker feathers to keep themselves warm.

Ptarmigan in winter

Some animals turn white as winter gets nearer. The stoat, Arctic fox, Arctic hare, lemming and ptarmigan all do this. They then become almost invisible against the snow.

White winter stoat

An Arctic fox hunting for . . .

. . . an Arctic hare

The animals all grow thicker fur and extra fat for the winter. Lemmings dig long tunnels in the snow just above the ground. From these tunnels they search for plants to feed on. Arctic hares look for food where the wind has blown the snow away from the plants. The Arctic fox has difficulty in finding enough to eat. Before winter begins it stores food. The fox hides dead birds and lemmings and birds' eggs beneath rocks and stones.

Only the Arctic ground squirrel of Canada sleeps for the winter. Polar bears do not hibernate but an adult female digs a cave deep in the snow. There she gives birth to her cubs. The males and younger female polar bears keep going all through the winter. In the sea the seals and fish are also active all the year round.

30

Summer in the Arctic

Summer in the Arctic lasts only about 3 months. For many days the sun never sets. The snow and ice melt away from much of the tundra. The ground is covered with a carpet of mosses, lichens and small plants.

But even in summer it is difficult to walk across the tundra. As we have seen, water from the melting ice cannot soak into the ground. The ground becomes marshy and dangerous. These marshes are the breeding grounds of huge swarms of mosquitoes and other insects.

A female grey wolf

Stampeding caribou

Caribou spend the summer on the tundra. They feed on the lichens and other plants. The broad hooves of the caribou stop them sinking into the snow in winter and into the marshes in summer. Wolves follow the caribou. They kill any sick or injured animals that cannot keep up with the herd.

More than 100 kinds of birds spend the summer on the tundra. Many have spent the winter in countries far to the south. These birds come to the tundra to nest. They include many kinds of ducks and geese and some swans. These birds feed themselves and their young on the insects and plants of the tundra.

Lesser snow geese feeding on the tundra

Innuits or Eskimos

A modern Innuit town, Kap Dan on Kulusuk Island

Until about 30 years ago, the only people living over much of the Arctic were Innuits or Eskimos. The Innuits live in Alaska, northern Canada and Greenland. They used to be experts at living in this severe climate. The Innuits made their living by hunting and fishing.

In the summer the Innuits lived in tents made of caribou skins. They ate the caribou meat. The caribou bones, teeth and antlers were made into bows, arrowheads, tools, jewellery, combs and toys.

Preparing caribou hide in an igloo

The Innuits' clothes were made from animal skins. They wore the furry side next to them. This trapped layers of air which helped to keep the Innuits warm. In the winter, when they were out hunting, the Innuits lived in igloos. An igloo is made of blocks of frozen snow formed into a dome shape. When they travelled from place to place the Innuits used husky dogs and sledges.

Building an igloo

Now only a few Innuits still hunt and fish. The old skills are dying out. When the Innuits do hunt they use rifles or harpoons. They use a snowmobile instead of a dog team. Most Innuits now live in permanent homes. Many of them have learned trades. They work for the oil companies, mines and airports in the area.

Greenland

Greenland is the second largest island in the world, after Australia. It is part of the Kingdom of Denmark. Most of Greenland lies within the Arctic Circle. It consists mainly of mountains and areas of high, flat land, or plateaux. The coast of Greenland is rocky, with many steep-sided inlets or fjords.

Snow falls on Greenland in every month of the year. But since the temperature rarely rises above freezing point, very little of the snow melts. The snow gets deeper and deeper and turns to ice. As a result, Greenland has the second largest ice-sheet in the world, after Antarctica. This ice is always moving. Near the sea the ice is gradually forced through gaps between the mountains. It forms glaciers.

Kayaks on the north-west coast of Greenland

Greenland is one of the homes of the Innuits. Nowadays, though, many of them have married Europeans. The chief work of the people of Greenland is fishing. The people live around the coast where the climate is less cold. Some valuable minerals have been found in Greenland. One of these is uranium which is used as a fuel in nuclear power stations. There is also a lot of aluminium ore, from which the metal aluminium is made.

Winter snowstorm

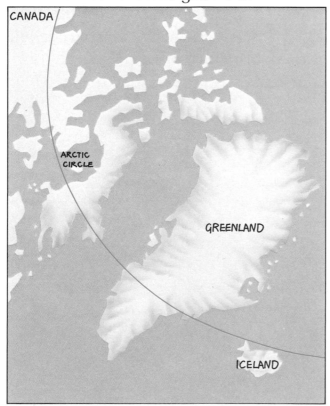

Alaska

The southern part of Alaska has a mild climate. This is because warm sea currents flow past this part of Alaska. Most of the people live in the southern part of Alaska. The interior and north of Alaska are very cold. It is mostly wild tundra country.

Fishing and mining make up the wealth of Alaska. The rivers teem with salmon. Many of these fish are canned and sent to other countries. Off the coast, fishing fleets catch cod, herrings and sardines. Gold, copper and platinum are the most important minerals in Alaska. But coal is also mined. Forestry and trapping animals for fur are also very important industries. In recent years a road has been built from the United States, through Canada, to Alaska. It is called the Alaska Highway.

Huge areas of Alaska have been made into national parks. But now oil has been discovered in Alaska. It

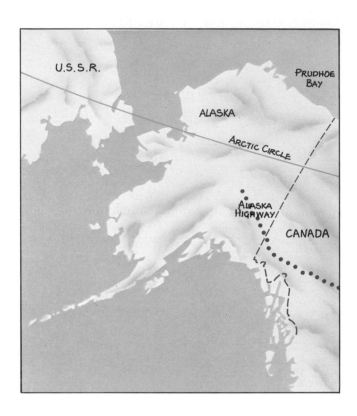

is produced at Prudhoe Bay. The hot oil is then piped across the mountains and valleys southwards. Ships collect the oil from the Valdez oil terminal. Alaska is one of the few wild areas left in the world. But now the search for oil is changing the landscape.

The Alaska Highway

Oil terminal at Tesoro

The Alaskan pipeline and permafrost

Already vast quantities of oil have been discovered in Alaska. As we have seen, to carry some of this oil away, a pipeline has been built. This is 1200 kilometres long. When the pipeline was being built, it was discovered how fragile the tundra is. Tracked vehicles could easily damage the delicate layer of plants and soil in the tundra. This thin layer of soil and plants protects the permafrost below. If the permafrost melts there is something like a gentle earthquake. If buildings or machines make the permafrost melt, the ground becomes soft. Buildings sink and oil pipelines crack.

To protect buildings in the Arctic they are built on gravel or pilings. Sometimes cold air is pumped

Hospital building raised away from the permafrost

underneath the buildings to stop the ground from thawing. Where the pipeline is above ground it is built on pilings. Where the pipeline is below ground, great care has to be taken to refill the trenches exactly as they were. Even so, it takes many years for the plants to grow again as they were. It was found that the pipeline had to be buried or raised where it crosses the route that the caribou follow on migration.

Caribou migrating under the trans-Alaska oil pipeline

Damaged tundra is slow to recover

Northern Canada

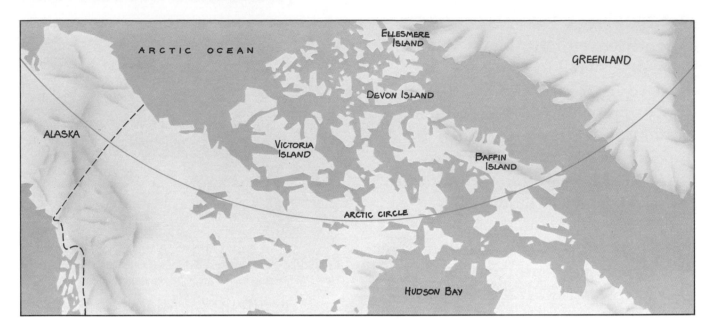

Much of northern Canada is a country of lakes and forests. But in the far north it is too cold even for trees. The whole area is tundra. Off the rugged north coast there are many islands. The largest of these are Baffin, Victoria, Devon and Ellesmere Islands. All the islands are cold and wind-swept. Permanent ice-sheets cover Baffin, Devon and Ellesmere Islands. And the waters around these islands are frozen for nine months of the year.

The native people of northern Canada are Innuits. In the past they made a living by hunting and trapping animals for their fur and meat. This was once the most important industry. But now the fur animals are reared on special farms. And the Canadian Innuits are learning new skills. Many now work as miners and mechanics in the new mines where a number of valuable minerals have been found.

There are few roads and railways in this part of Canada. Aircraft are used to search for the minerals. They are often fitted with skis so that they can land on the frozen snow.

Twin-engine Otter aircraft on skis

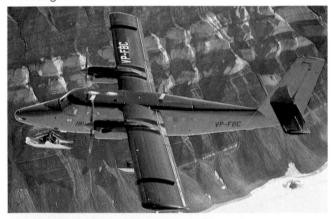

The shoreline tundra of Victoria island

Lapland

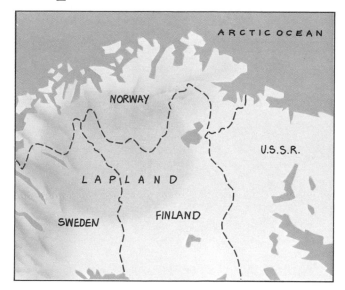

A Lapp family cooking a meal inside a traditional tent

Lapland is the name given to a large area of tundra country. It is partly in northern Finland and partly in northern Norway and Sweden.

The people of Lapland are called Lapps. They used to be true nomads. Nomads are wanderers. They do not have a settled home. The nomadic Lapps keep reindeer.

The nomadic Lapps follow their herds of reindeer to the places where the reindeer can find food. They spend the summer on the northern tundra. But in the early autumn the Lapps and their reindeer begin the long journey towards the lowlands further south. They set up camp near the forests where there is plenty of wood for fuel. The Lapps sleep in tents made of reindeer skins. The reindeer also provide the Lapps with meat and milk. And their clothes are made from reindeer hides. Some of the reindeer are also used to pull sledges and to carry loads. The two biggest enemies of the Lapps are wolves and blizzards.

Today, most Lapps earn their living from fishing, forestry or working in the mines. They now live in timber houses. But a few Lapps still lead a nomadic life.

Herding reindeer

A Lapp preparing reindeer hide

Siberia

Siberia is the northern part of Russia. It receives only about 13 centimetres of rain and snow a year. The whole area is an icy desert. The summers are brief and the winters long and bitterly cold.

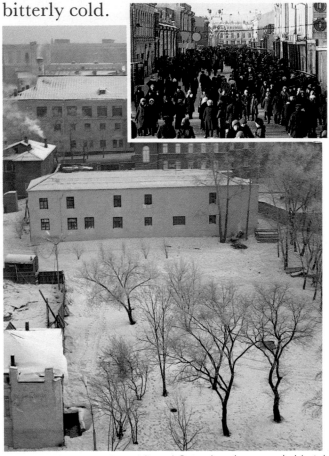

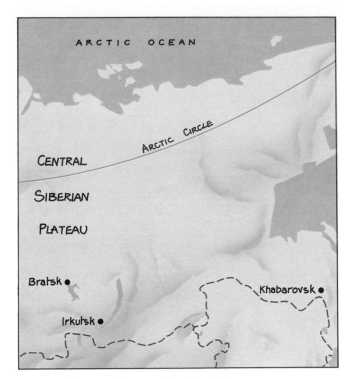

Winter in Khabarovsk and (inset) Saturday shoppers in Irkutsk

For centuries few people lived in Siberia because of this climate. But Siberia has a large number of valuable minerals beneath its surface. In places coal, iron ore, diamonds, gold, oil and natural gas are found. In 1928 the Russian government decided to mine these minerals. At first, prisoners were forced to work in the mines. But now workers are offered high wages and long holidays to work in Siberia. New

towns have been built. There are power stations to make electricity. But most people stay in Siberia only a few years. Then they move to places with a better climate.

The largest rivers of Siberia flow into the Arctic Ocean. For much of the year they are frozen solid. Special ships called ice-breakers are used to keep the channels open in summer. This allows other ships to get through to the river ports.

Pulp Mill at Bratsk

The Ice Ages

The polar regions are very cold. They are the coldest places on Earth. But long ago nearly one-third of all the land on Earth was covered with ice. This is because the Earth was once a much colder place than it is today. The Earth was in the Ice Age. There were at least four of these Ice Ages. In between there were warmer spells.

During the Ice Ages all of Canada and much of the United States were covered with ice. Britain was covered with ice as far south as London and the River Thames. Norway, Sweden, Finland, Denmark and the northern parts of Germany, Poland and Russia were also beneath the ice. In

the south, the Antarctic ice-sheet was also much larger than it is today.

When the Earth became warmer, about 10,000 years ago, much of the ice melted. Where glaciers had been, U-shaped valleys were left. Some of these valleys filled with water and lakes formed. There were low hills of clay and rocks which had been pushed along by the glaciers. These now form valuable farmland.

With the melting of the ice, the sea-level rose. Some of the land was flooded. In some parts of the world there are the remains of forests under the sea. These trees were drowned when the sea-level rose.

Do you remember?

1 What countries does the Arctic Circle run through?

2 Why is little water to be seen in the Arctic Ocean?

3 What is the North Pole like?

4 What is the tundra?

5 How do the flowering plants on the tundra stop themselves being blown away?

6 What is permafrost?

7 What happens to the rocks on the tundra when the water caught in their crevices and cracks freezes?

8 What do we call tame caribou?

9 What do lemmings do when winter comes?

10 How does the Arctic fox prepare for winter?

11 Name three Arctic animals which turn white when winter comes.

12 How long does summer in the Arctic last?

13 Why is the ground so wet on the tundra in summer?

14 Why do so many birds of different kinds come to the tundra in summer?

15 How did the Innuits make their living until about 30 years ago?

16 What kind of work do the Innuits do now?

17 Why did the Innuits wear animal skins with the furry side next to the skin?

18 To which country does Greenland belong?

19 What kind of fish are caught in the rivers of Alaska?

20 How is the oil from Alaska carried to the port?

21 What happens if the permafrost melts?

22 When buildings are put up in Alaska, what is done to protect the permafrost?

23 Name two islands off the coast of northern Canada.

24 Where are most fur animals reared nowadays?

25 Of which countries is Lapland a part?

26 What are nomads?

27 What animals do the Lapps keep?

28 What is done to attract workers to Siberia?

29 What were the Ice Ages?

30 What happened to the sea when the ice melted at the end of the Ice Ages?

Things to do

1 Keep a weather notebook

Keep a weather notebook. Every day write down what the weather is like and what the temperature is. Look at the temperature at the same time each day.

2 What happens when water freezes?

Completely fill a plastic bottle with water and screw the top on tightly. Put the bottle in the freezing compartment of the refrigerator or in a deep-freeze overnight. What has happened to the bottle the next day? Why is this?

3 A project about the animals and birds of the polar regions

Choose either the Arctic or Antarctic. Make a book about the birds and animals of your chosen polar region. See that there are plenty of pictures to go in your book. Say how each of the animals or birds feeds and how it is adapted to living in this cold part of the world.

4 A scrapbook of pictures of clothes

Make a scrapbook of pictures of clothes. Collect only pictures of clothes people wear in very hot countries and in very cold countries. Divide your pictures into these two groups. What differences do you see? What similarities are there?

5 How do different colours absorb the sun's rays?

Take two similar thermometers and two sheets of paper, one black and the other white, but both the same size.

Lay the two thermometers near to each other in sunshine. What is the temperature?

Cover one thermometer with a sheet of black paper and the other with a sheet of white paper. Leave them in the sunshine for 15 to 30 minutes. Now quickly remove

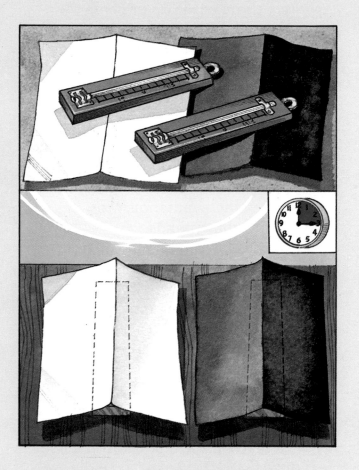

the two sheets of paper and see what temperature each of the two thermometers says. Under which sheet of paper was it the hotter? Under which sheet of paper was it the cooler? Which colour paper absorbs more of the sun's rays?

What colour clothes would it be best to wear if you were cold? What colour clothes would you wear if you were hot?

Can you think of one reason why the summers are warmer in the Arctic tundra where the snow melts, than they are in the Antarctic where the snow does not melt?

If you cannot do this experiment in sunshine, you can always do it using the heat and light from a desk lamp or table lamp. But make sure that the light falls equally on both sheets of paper.

6   Keeping warm   For this experiment, you need two tins both the same size, with lids. You also need two thermometers.

Make a hole in the lid of each tin. Make the hole big enough for a thermometer to go through.

Stand the tins on a tray or on several layers of newspaper on the table. Take the lids off. Wrap a piece of woollen cloth around one tin and cotton wool around the other. Fasten these materials with Sellotape or rubber bands.

Ask your teacher to fill each tin from a kettle of hot water. There should be the same amount of water in each tin and it should be at the same temperature. Carefully put the lid on each tin and put a thermometer through the hole in the lid.

Take the temperature of the water in each tin every 10 minutes. Make a graph to show how the water in each tin cooled. Use a different coloured line for each tin.

Which tin cools the quickest? Which tin cools the slowest? Which would make the warmest clothing, cotton wool or woollen cloth?

Now do the experiment again with two other kinds of materials wrapped around the tins. If you can, try a piece of fur. Which is the warmest kind of material you can find?

7   A model igloo   If you can, get some white polystyrene ceiling tiles. Cut one or two of the tiles into pieces about 2 centimetres square. Use these pieces to make a model igloo. You could either glue the pieces together or fasten them with pins.

Use one of the ceiling tiles as a base for your igloo.

You could, if you wish, make hills and valleys of snow around your igloo using plaster of Paris.

Make lists of the trees, buildings and places which are North, South, East and West of where you are standing.

You can make a very simple compass if you have a bar magnet. Cut a strip of cloth about 3 centimetres wide and 15 centimetres long. Make a hole in the centre of each end of the piece of cloth. Take a short length of string and tie one end into each hole in the cloth. You have now made a sling.

Place the bar magnet in the sling. Hang the sling up by the loop of string away from metal objects. Which way does the magnet point? Push the magnet slightly. What happens? Does the magnet always point the same way?

8   Make paper snowflakes   Take a sheet of white or silver paper. Lay a saucer or jar lid on the paper and cut around it. Fold the circle of paper into six and cut pieces out of it. When you unfold the paper it will look like a snowflake. Mount your snowflakes on black paper or make mobiles with them.

9   Draw pictures   Draw pictures, or make collages, showing the Arctic tundra in summer and in winter.

10   Using a compass   If you walk in the polar regions, it is essential to take a compass in case there is a snowstorm and you lose your way.

Learn how a compass works. Take a compass into the garden or playground. Set the compass so that the North on the scale and the point of the needle are both pointing in the same direction.

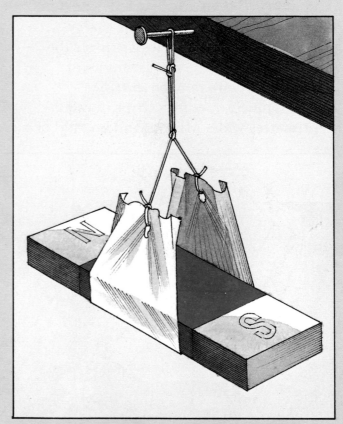

11   An expedition to the polar regions   Imagine you are going on an expedition to either the North or South Pole. Write a story about your adventures. Do not forget to say what food, clothes and equipment you took. Say what the weather was like and what difficulties you met with.

12 Make some ice lollies

Take the ice-cube tray from the refrigerator. Make up some fruit drinks by adding squash or lemonade powder to water in a glass or jug. Stir the mixture thoroughly. Fill the compartments of the ice-cube tray exactly to the top with fruit drink.

Carefully put the ice-cube tray back in the freezing compartment of the fridge. When the ice is half-set, cover the tray with foil and push a clean lolly stick into each compartment. How long do the ice lollies take to form? What mixture of water and squash or lemonade powder gives the best tasting lollies?

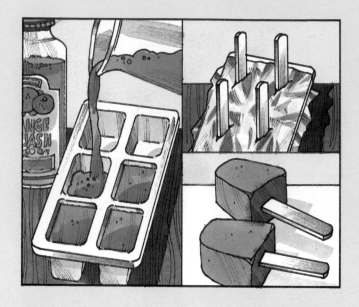

13 Make a model polar scene

Use a piece of wire-netting as the foundation for your scene. Crumple the wire netting into the shape you want (Careful the wire may be sharp!).

Cut a newspaper into strips about 2 centimetres wide. Mix a small bowlful of thin cold-water glue or wallpaper paste. Wet the strips of newspaper with the glue or paste. Cover the wire netting with the strips. See that all the wire netting is covered with several layers of newspaper.

Leave your model on one side. When the newspaper has dried out completely, paint your model. Make some cardboard cut-out animals to go in your scene.

44

14 Birds which migrate

Find out about the journeys of some migrating birds which spend part of their lives in the polar regions. The world record traveller is probably the Arctic tern. Some of these birds nest on the Arctic tundra and then fly south to spend the rest of the year down near the Antarctic Ocean. Some other birds you might think about are redwings, fieldfares, pink-footed geese, black-headed gulls and Bewick's swans.

Find a map of the world. Glue it on to a larger piece of carboard.

Choose two or three birds which migrate to or from the polar regions. Make small coloured drawings of each of the birds you have chosen. Cut out each drawing and stick a pin through it. Pin the drawing of the bird to one of the countries where it might spend the summer. Use a bird book to help you with this. Place another pin in one of the areas where the bird might spend the winter. Join the two pins by a coloured thread.

The thread shows the journey the bird might take if it flies in a straight line. Try and find out roughly how far it flies. What countries does it pass through? What are these countries like? Find out which seas, mountains, rivers, lakes and deserts the bird passes over. Do these things for the other birds you have chosen as well.

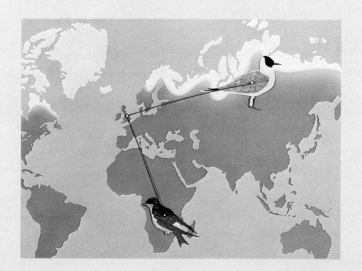

Arctic Tern (breeding plumage)

Redwing

Black-headed Gull (breeding plumage)

Fieldfare

Pink-footed Goose

Bewick's swan

Things to find out

1   Choose an animal which lives in the polar regions. Find out all you can about it. How is it able to survive in the polar regions? Collect as many pictures as you can of your chosen animal. Make a book about your animal.

2   Lichens are simple plants that grow in the polar regions. What is unusual about a lichen? Where else do lichens grow? Why are there not many lichens in towns?

3   Why are people so interested in the oil and other minerals in the Arctic and Antarctic now, when they have not been particularly interested in them in the past?

4   In the polar regions litter is becoming a problem. This is because the litter takes much longer to rot away. Find out why this should be.

5   Nowadays the fur to make fur coats often comes from animals reared on special farms. In what ways is this better than the old way of trapping wild life?

46

6   In some parts of the tundra in spring, people search for the nests of eider duck. What do these people collect from the nests and what do they use it for?

7   Why do the people living in the tundra areas of the Arctic not grow crops such as wheat, oats, barley and potatoes?

8   Find out about icebreakers. Why do these ships have to be stronger than ordinary ships? Which part of an icebreaker needs to be strongest? Why?

9   Find out which animals hibernate in your country. Why do you think so few animals hibernate in the Arctic?

10   What do you think happened to the wildlife in the Arctic when the Eskimos learned to use rifles instead of harpoons?

11   Which country does Alaska belong to? Which country owned Alaska previously? When was it sold and for how much?

12   Was the area where you live covered by ice during the Ice Age? You might be able to tell if you look at the map on page 39   If the area where you live was covered by ice, what evidence of it can you find?

13   What are snow-shoes? How do they work? Some animals of the tundra, like polar bears and caribou have extra wide feet. What advantage is this to animals which live where there is a lot of snow?

14   Fifty years ago the musk ox in the Arctic was nearly extinct. This was because the rifle had made killing so easy. Find out what was done to save the musk ox from extinction. What are the musk ox used for by people?

Glossary

Here are the meanings of some words which you might have met for the first time in this book.

Antarctica: the continent surrounding the South Pole.

Arctic: the northern polar regions.

Atmosphere: the big layer of air which surrounds the Earth.

Continent: one of the seven large pieces of land on the Earth's surface.

Equator: the giant imaginary circle around the centre of the Earth.

Fjord: a steep-sided valley worn out by a glacier and flooded by the sea.

Food chain: a series of plants and animals linked together by their food and what eats them. Food chains always start with plants.

Geyser: a spring which sends out hot water and steam.

Glacier: a large river of ice which flows down a valley.

Hibernation: sleeping for the winter.

Ice Ages: the periods of time, thousands of years ago, when the Earth was much colder than it is today.

Icebergs: large blocks of ice which float in the sea around the polar regions. The ice was originally formed on land.

Ice breaker: a special ship which breaks through ice to keep channels open.

Ice sheet: a huge sheet of ice and snow covering Greenland or Antarctica. During the Ice Ages a huge ice sheet covered large parts of Europe and North America.

Ice shelf: an ice sheet that has reached the sea and is floating.

Lava: the hot, liquid rock which comes out of a volcano.

Migration: the journeys of animals, birds and people from one country to another, or one part of a country to another, usually in search of food or a warmer climate.

Mineral salts: the chemical substances which plants obtain from the soil or water and which they use as food.

National Park: a large area of land over which special care is taken to see that the beautiful scenery is not spoilt and where the rare plants and animals are protected.

Nomads: people who roam from place to place looking for food for their animals, instead of having just one home.

Pack ice: a large area of floating ice formed on the sea where the sea water has frozen.

Permafrost: ground which is permanently frozen.

Plankton: the minute plants and animals which float in sea water. Plankton is food for many fishes, whales and other sea animals.

Plateaux: areas of high, level land.

Polar regions: the areas around the North and South Poles.

Poles: North and South Poles. The ends of the Earth's imaginary axis on which it spins.

Tundra: the treeless lands around the Arctic Ocean.

Volcano: a weak part of the Earth's crust through which molten rock or lava from inside the Earth comes out.

Index